Feel

I feel as high as a kite,
But as low as the bottom of the ocean.
I feel like I'm going slowly
while everyone's in motion.
I'm feeling like I want to die
but part of me wants to live.
I have these feelings of sadness,
like what more do I have to give?

What I Lost

I lost all hope,
and found it hard to see.
How long can I live like this,
how long can I be me?
I lost my motivation,
and don't want to go out.
All that I do,
is sit home and pout.
I want to feel better,
and I need some help.
But this hopelessness is big,
and so small I felt.
I'm trying I tell them,
but sometimes they don't see,
how hard it is to be,
in the mind I have in me.

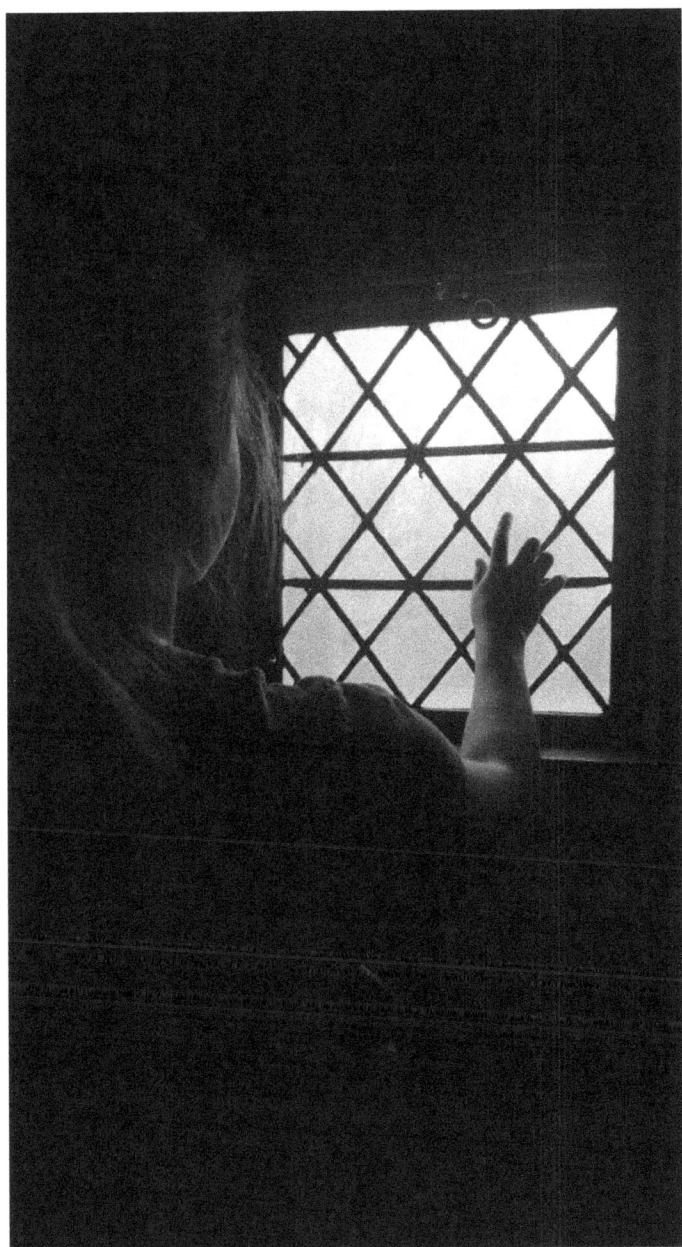

That Little Girl

As the rain falls,
I start to wonder.
About the little girl,
who used to be filled with wonder.
That little girl who had no stress.
The little girl, with that little dress.
Now the little girl is grown,
now filled with stress.
That little girl who used to wear
that little red dress.
Now she cares too much,
and holds the weight of the world.
She doesn't believe herself,

like the little girl would.

I Write

I write about sadness.
I write about feeling.
I write to let it out.
I write about dealing,
with all these emotions
that I can't explain.
I write it on paper,
to let out the pain.
I keep it inside,
and let it out with words.
I'm waiting for the day,
that I can say I'm cured.

I'm Home
Now that I'm home,
back to the same old town.
I feel like crying,
I feel so down.
I want to spread my wings,
but it's so hard to do,
when you feel like you're drowning,
when you feel so blue.
I don't know what to do,
and I don't know why.
I feel so alone,
in this mind of mine.
I just want to sleep,
and never wake up.
I just want to be able,
to sit there and cut.

Weak

I feel so weak,
and the urge is so strong.
I know it's not ok.
I know it is wrong.

It's becoming hard to breathe,
and I'm sinking once again.
I don't know how to explain this.
I don't know where to begin.

It's like I'm on this mountain,
and I just can't reach the top.
I want this feeling to go away.
I want them to stop.

It seems impossible,
to escape my mind.
This mountain,
seems impossible to climb.

Racing Thoughts

I'm alone with my thoughts,
and it's terrifying.
My mind won't stop,
it won't stop racing.
Dark clouds are floating over me,
and I can't see the sun.
I'm exhausted,
and I'm done,
dealing with these thoughts
that are killing me inside.
But like a wise man once said,
the truth lies.
And the truth is things will get better.
Believing that is hard.
I'm losing control of my mind.
I don't know where to start.
How to feel better.
How to deal with what I have.
How to deal with emotions.
How to deal with being sad.
What to believe.
Where to find,
the strength to take control,
of this mind.

Forget it all

Smoke to let it out.
Cut to release the pain.
Run to let off some steam.
Brush it off with paint.

Drive to forget.
Listen to music to escape.
Your feelings are valid,
they are not fake.

Write to put feelings on paper.
Walk to shake it off.
Dance to feel good.
Anything to forget it all.

The Gloomy Weather

The gloomy weather reflects how I feel.
And I'm told to go on, like it's no big deal.
Told to put my feelings aside, and be ok.
Like it's so easy to put these feelings away.
But the truth in the matter is that it's not.
Not so simple to live with what I've got.
To live feeling the way I do.
To live with all my shitty moods.
I'm so tired and I don't know how to cope.
Other than putting that blade to my skin,
feeling no hope.
I wish it was as easy as a switch.
Easy as climbing out of this ditch,
that I can't seem to get out of.
I wish I could just shove,
these feeling aside,
that are tearing me apart.
But I just don't know where to begin,
where to even start.
How to push these feelings aside.
How to handle being alive.

Monsters

Tears in the night,
keep creeping inside.
The monsters in my head,
make me question being alive.
Staying awake at night,
just to hear the monsters speak.
I have no strength over them.
They make me feel so weak.
They talk about things that
I can't explain.
I lose sight of the sun,
I only see the rain.
I have no control,
of the things they say.
But I keep going on.
Living day by day.

Who Are You?

Who are you?
when no one's looking?
Who are you?
What mask are you putting?
To make sure no one sees,
who you truly are.
With all those scars,
running down your arm.
Hide it from everyone,
and leave it unsaid.
Don't show anyone,
what you really do at your bed.
When you put those razors to your skin,
and start to bleed.
Because if you tell them,
that'll just leave.
Leave you all alone,
with all of your thoughts.
Because they really don't know,
how hard you fought.
And then when they get the call,
that you're no longer here,
They'll regret what they did,
and it all becomes so clear.

The Monster in my Head

In the Halloween spirit,
I go to hide.
From the scary things,
that are inside.
The scariest place
is not the monster under my bed,
but the ones that lurk,
inside my head.
That creep in places,
where you can't find.
They creep in places,
that are in my mind.

Don't Let Anyone Know

It's hard for me,
to let my feelings show.
It's easier to just,
not let anyone know.
Put on a happy face.
Don't let anyone in.
Take it out on myself,
by breaking my skin.
Let the blood drip,
and watch as I cry.
Sometimes it seems easier,
to just say goodbye.

A Trip to the Hospital

So I'm back in this place,
filled with white walls.
Where I thought I'd never be.
I tried to end this life of mine,
then found it hard to see.
The ambulance rushed to my house,
and the police said do you know why I'm here.
I said yes I know I tried to die,
and then I was filled with fear.
I was rushed to this place filled with medicines,
doctors, nurses and IVs.
Again I'm back to this same old environment,

where I came to learn about me.

Weak

I feel so weak,
and the urge is so strong.
I know it's not ok.
I know it's wrong.
It's getting hard to breathe.
And I'm sinking once again.
I don't know how to explain,
or where to begin.
It's like I'm on this mountain,
and I just can't climb to the top.
I wish these feelings would go away.
I hope for these feelings to stop.

I Act

I act like I'm ok,
but inside it really hurts.
I try so much,
but nothing seems to work.
I act like I'm alright,
but it always feels so bad,
like I'm on this long flight,
that's going to crash,
and fall to the ground.
It's like I'm lost
and will never be found.
I can't seem to change,
no matter what I do.
I'm always feeling bad.
I'm always feeling blue.
I'm trying,
I really, truly am.
But this plane will be ok,
and it's going to land.

When They Ask

They ask me what's wrong,
then they ask me why.
I hate being asked,
because then it makes me cry.
I don't know what to say.
I don't always know,
every time I'm asked,
I just want to go,
run away from everything,
and be someone else.
I can't explain why,
that's just how I felt.
I learned my feelings are valid,
but that's so hard to believe.
I just want to go,
run away and leave,
from these thoughts that I have,
I want to escape my mind.
I don't want to be sad,
I just want to be fine.
Eventually I hope,
I'll find my way soon.
But until then,
I'll escape in my tunes.

Questions

Who do I tell my secrets to?
What do I even say?
Where can I find the words?
When will I find a better day?
Why do I feel the way I do?
How can I get past it?
These questions,
make me want to give up.
They make me want to quit.

Halloween

Skeletons and ghosts,
are in my head.
Monsters that scare,
beneath my bed.
Pumpkins and costumes,
are all around.
On this Halloween day,
where scarecrows and witches
all surround.

Dream Big

Dream big.
Expect little.
Be kind
and be civil.
Don't let anyone tell you,
you can't.
When you fall,
get up and stand.
Fall seven times,
stand up eight.
When there's no one around,
create.
Create your own path
and don't get yourself down.
Put on that smile.
Don't always frown.
You can do it,
I know you can.
When things don't go your way,
get up and re-plan.

Depression

I lost all confidence,
and all my self-esteem.
It's like I'm in a river
swimming opposite of the stream .
I lost who I used to be,
and now I'm someone else.
I don't know how to become
my own true self.
I don't know who myself is
and I lost all control.
This depression has taken over
and my life it stole.
I wish I could reverse time
to a simpler place.
To where I didn't have a care in the world.
When I didn't feel like a waste of space.
But that's impossible, I know.
I have to live in the now.
I don't know how to do that.
But I'll figure out how.

Take Me Away

Take me away to a better place.
Where there's so much good to embrace.
Where I can see a better day than today.
To a place where the sun shines on your face.
Take me to a better place.
Where the flowers grow in the shade.
Where I won't be afraid.
To a place where my feelings disappear.
To where I have no fear.
One day I will come to this place.
A place where I feel safe.

My Skin

Smoke fills my lungs,
as I ponder my life.
As it's crumbling down to pieces,
I think about that knife.
It seems like my friend,
when I have no one else.
When I'm alone at night,
and there's no one there to help.
When no one's around,
I think about my skin.
How it breaks so easy,
when the knife is paper thin.
But I'll put down that knife one day,
and learn to let it go.
I'll learn to do better.
I'll learn to let myself grow.

Nightmare
I'm in a nightmare,
and I can't wake up.
If I told you what's on my mind,
you'd think I was nuts.
People think I make it up.
It's all in my head they say.
It's all for attention,
like I'd want to be this way.
I would give anything
not to feel the way I do.
But they don't see,
except for a rare few.
I wouldn't wish this on anyone,
because this is torture.
And all I think about,
is how I will beat this disorder?

Fast

Cars and planes
how fast they go
while everyone's in motion.
All these feelings
deep inside.
I can't count my emotions.
Happy, sad, angry, hurt.
All of these I feel.
How hard it is to feel ok.
How hard it is to heal.

Don't Stop

Keep on writing.
Keep on going.
Don't stop moving.
Don't stop growing.

Hold your head high.
Keep your hopes up.
Create your way through.
Get your mind out of that rut.

Keep on thinking.
because thinking is living.
If you stop yourself from dreaming,
you don't know what you're missing.

Distract Yourself

Put away your feelings,
in a little box.
Put in the emotions,
put away your thoughts.
Be mindful of what you're doing.
Don't act on your feelings.
Distract yourself from pain.
Focus on your healing.
Let the thoughts slip from your mind,
like they are slipping on ice.
When you think you're falling back,
think twice.
Think twice about your actions.
Listen to some music.
Anything to distract yourself.
It can be therapeutic.

What I'm Worth

I'm left out.
I'm just old news.
I'm nothing more than memories,
that have already been used.
I'm not worth the time.
I'm a puzzle with missing pieces.
I'm not me anymore.
I'm an essay without the thesis.
If I had another chance,
I'd be more than I am today.
Or maybe I'd be worse,
or maybe even the same.
But another chance I'll take,
to be a better me.
I'm not worth the time,
that I can guarantee.

Breathe

Breathe in, breathe out.
Be thankful. Don't pout.
Inhale the good, exhale the bad.
Your feelings are valid;
you have a right to be sad.
Push your feelings to the side.
I know it's difficult to do.
`But it's better to let it out,
than do something you can't undo.
When you feel so hopeless,
and don't know where to turn,
think about your reasons to live,
before you cut or burn.
Before you get to that point,
where you feel as low as you can feel.
When you feel like you're losing control,
go ahead and take the wheel.

My Broken Heart

You will cut yourself

on the pieces of my broken heart.

I will hurt you,

and tear you apart.

I can't help myself.

And I can't help you.

So leave while you can.

Or I'll make you feel blue.

I'll bring you down with me,

because I can't help myself.

Put away your feelings for me,

in a box on a shelf.

Never touch it again,

if you don't want to bleed.

Please don't come close.

Please just leave.

The Ticking Clock

The clock is ticking,

and I have no time to get up this mountain

that's impossible to climb.

I don't know if I'll be able to get to the top,

unless the clock freezes,

and the ticker stops.

I have no time to reach to the point.

And if I don't reach it,

I'll just disappoint.

Everyone around me

is waiting for me to get there.

But I can't breathe anymore.

I'm gasping for air.

I'm panting and pushing,

to get to where I need to be.

But the place where I need to be

is impossible to see.

I'll reach the top eventually,

but maybe not in time.

I hope I'll reach the point,

during this lifetime.

Hidden

I'm hidden behind words,

words that make sentences.

Sentences that make paragraphs,

paragraphs that create emphasis.

I'm hidden behind journals,

that are written with pen.

There are no mistakes.

It leaves you in suspense.

I'm hidden in this depression.

It's becoming the new me.

I'm not who I was.

Not who I used to be.

Missing You

I'm trying to drink you away,

to get you off my mind.

But as each day goes by,

I miss you more after all this time.

I know you're not coming back for me,

no matter how much I need you here.

Until I get to see you,

I'll just drink all these beers,

until I forget you even left.

To distract myself from this emptiness.

I'll remember when you were here.

And when I could feel your happiness.

I'll hide under the covers,

to forget how much I miss you.

I'll cover myself from these feelings,

because I feel that's all I can do.

Gone in an Instant

As I sit here in the cold,

I think about your smile.

How I miss it so much.

I haven't seen it in a while.

As I shiver from the wind,

I think about your eyes.

How when you left,

It hit me by surprise.

You were gone in an instant.

One day you're here, the next you're not.

So I hold on to these memories,

Because it's all that I've got.

Roses are red

Roses are red

Violets are blue

But roses have thorns

And so do you.

These thorns will cut deep,

And leave you with blood.

As red as the roses,

That represents love.

Sinking

I'm sinking and I won't float.

I'm drowning, I have no hope.

I'm tired but I can't stop.

I'm panting to get to the top.

I'm climbing up this hill.

I'm standing on the edge to feel the thrill.

I'm running away from me.

I'm looking but I can't see.

I'm bleeding to know I'm alive.

I'm slow but I will arrive.

I'm walking but I'm standing still.

I'm drowning in all of this guilt.

I'm sad and happy at the same time.

I'm angry but I am still kind.

I'm lonely with people around.

I'm yelling but make no sound.

I'm screaming for someone to help.

I'm hiding from what I've felt.

I'm boiling but I am so cold.

I'm lost and uncontrolled.

It'll get better is what I'm told.

But I'm looking for a hand to hold.

Behind

I'll be behind that camera to snap that picture.

I'll be behind that gun but won't pull the trigger.

I'll be painting my way through to stop from thinking.

I'll swim to the top to stop myself from sinking.

I'll be writing poetry to ease my mind.

I'll prevent myself from getting out of line.

Hopefully I'll be ok in the future.

I won't pull the trigger. I won't be the shooter.

Roller Coaster

Like a roller coaster, I go up and down.

I smile when I'm happy; When I'm sad I frown.

I'll be ok eventually, but not right now.

I'm just afraid I'll fall to the ground.

I'll fall deep in this hole and reach rock bottom.

On a really dark day in the cold night of autumn.

I'll fall so hard and hit the world like a drum.

This depression has taken over

and it's what I've become.

One day I'm hot, the next I'm cold.

That's going to change is what I am told.

Eventually I'll soar with the wind and fly like a bird.

But right now I can't because my vision is blurred.

I'll die like the roses on a really cold day.

I can't help but think it'll happen that way.

Day by Day

Take it day by day.

Don't move too fast,

If you want these memories

And moments to last.

Take it step by step,

Like you're going up stairs.

I know it's difficult

Because life isn't fair.

Cross things off your list

One at a time.

Don't become overwhelmed

It's your time to shine.

Christmas

Starry nights

Christmas lights

Sleigh bells ding

Joyful smiles

Days worth while

Christmas trees

Memories

The season has arrived

With present surprises

Whispers

I hear the typewriter tapping in my mind.

As the letter flow on the paper, with word so kind.

I hear the whispers outside in the night.

They speak of bad things that leave me in fright.

I hear the wind blowing softly.

I hear the monsters in my head constantly.

They speak of death and how nice it would be.

They speak of how it's impossible to feel recovery.

I can't see the light at the end of the tunnel.

I see the world around me start to crumble.

Write

It's never too late to become you again.

You can become whoever you want with a paper and a pen.

Live in another world and create the new you.

You can do anything you set your mind to.

You can fly or dream or even meet your goals.

Make you to be an inspiration, and fill in the holes.

The holes that are in your heart and become someone great.

Write it all on paper, there's no time to wait.

Fight

I'll fight this battle

I'll win this war

I'll spread my wings

Just watch me soar

I'll do my best

I'll be ok

I'll fight so hard

I'll find my way

www.ingramcontent.com/pod-product-compliance
Lightning Source LLC
LaVergne TN
LVHW051430080426
835508LV00022B/3327